DAVID BENNETT COHEN
TEACHES
Blues Piano

A Hands-on Course in Traditional Blues Piano

— Featuring a Comprehensive Audio Lesson —

Dedicated to Devin Nelson Bischoff

PLAYBACK+
Speed • Pitch • Balance • Loop

To access audio visit:
www.halleonard.com/mylibrary

Enter Code
3326-2145-1551-5048

Cover Photo by David Burton

Audio Editor: Ted Orr

Mastered by: Ted Orr at
Nevessa Productions, Woodstock, NY

ISBN 978-0-7935-6257-2

HOMESPUN®

EXCLUSIVELY DISTRIBUTED BY
HAL•LEONARD®
7777 W. BLUEMOUND RD. P.O. BOX 13819 MILWAUKEE, WI 53213

Table of Contents

This book contains music examples and instructional songs, and the audio examples are labeled with track icons (◆) for the ease of locating the corresponding tracks. The remaining tracks listed here contain detailed explanation and instruction for these songs.

Audio instruction makes it easy! Find the section of the lesson you want with the press of a finger; play that segment over and over until you've mastered it; easily skip over parts you've already mastered; listen with the best possible audio fidelity; follow along track-by-track with the book.

Introduction

The goal of this book is to get you started playing blues piano. Toward this end I have begun with two simple concepts, the shuffle rhythm and the slow blues. I have provided several simple solos and a scale for improvisation.

Blues is a form of folk music, and as such, comes from an aural tradition, meaning that the music is played differently each time it is played. The solos that I have included, although written, are only meant as a starting point. Once you learn the solos, think about changing them. Don't be concerned so much with improvising the entire verse, but more about changing one phrase, or even one note, at a time. Also try incorporating the various riffs, or musical phrases, into your improvising. The idea is to try and build a large "bag of tricks" that you can dip into whenever you play. Try to think of the "minor blues scale" as a starting point.

Learning the music is technical. Playing it so that it sounds good is up to your taste, facility and imagination. Play everything slowly at first. Count your measures. It's more important for the music to sound good than to put a lot of notes in it, although sometimes a lot of notes will sound good. The shuffle rhythm, when played correctly, is irresistibly danceable. The slow blues can be very emotional, covering a wide range of feelings from sadness to determination. As a result, it can be a real catharsis.

Blues is a wonderful form of music that I've always been drawn to. It somehow touches a fundamental need that I seem to have. I'm certainly not alone in this feeling. Blues has and always will have its dedicated followers. Perhaps it is because blues comes from suffering that is so joyful and therefore attractive to so many people.

I strongly urge you to listen to as much blues piano as you can. Some piano players that I recommend are Professor Longhair, Otis Spann, Memphis Slim, Tuts Washington, all of the Pinetops (Smith, Perkins, etc.), Allen Toussain, Dr. John, Barry Goldberg (if you can find some of his recordings with Michael Bloomfield or Steve Miller). Mark Naftalin (from Paul Butterfield Blues Band), Corky Siegel, Huey "Piano" Smith, Fats Domino, Jerry Lee Lewis, and the list goes on.

As a teacher, some students come to me because they feel that they have reached a stalemate. They just don't seem to be able to play anything new. But everyone reaches plateaus at one time or another. No matter how much you know, there is always more to learn. It's amazing to me the number of permutations that can be made with just a few notes.

Only a small percent of improvisational music is going to come from inspiration. Mostly you are going to have to work at it. The more you play, the more you will learn and the more you will discover different ways to play the same notes.

Always try to listen to what you are playing. Exercise and develop your taste. If it sounds good, keep it. If you are playing something wrong, then unlearning it is learning something new. It doesn't matter whether you are playing at home or at a gig, every time you play you are practicing.

So, I guess that the best advice I can give is to keep playing.

David Bennett Cohen

Blues Basics

4 C Major Scale

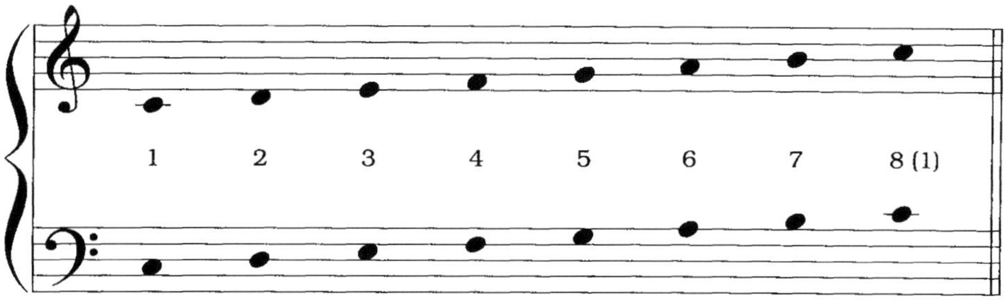

5 Blues Form: I - IV - V

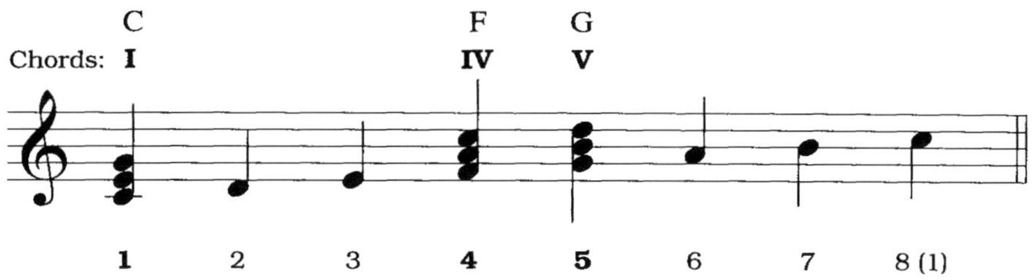

Shuffle Rhythm – Triplets

6 Rhythms

Example 1 – Shuffle Rhythm (Traditional Blues)

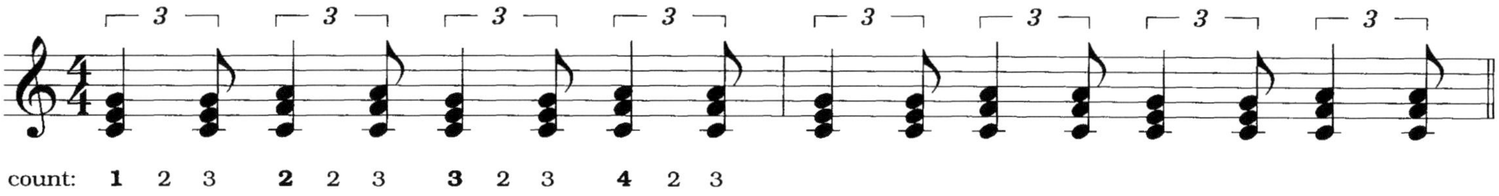

Example 2 – Straight Time Rhythm (Rock 'n' Roll)

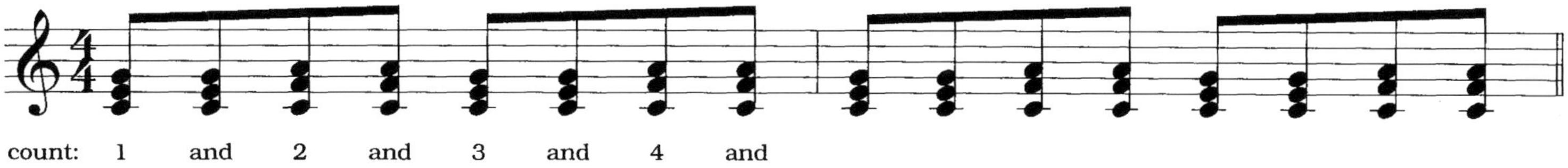

7 Left Hand Rhythm

8 Combining Left and Right Hands

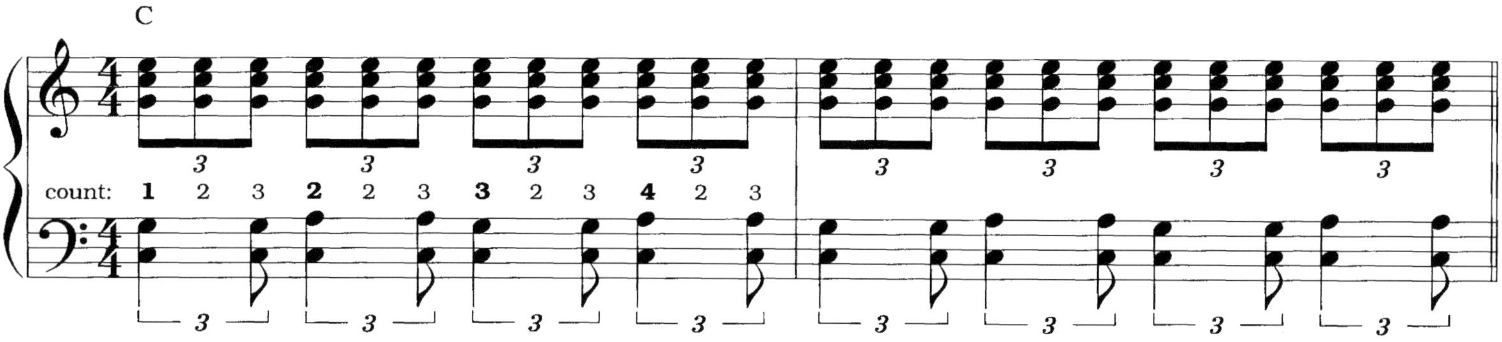

9 12 Bar Blues Form

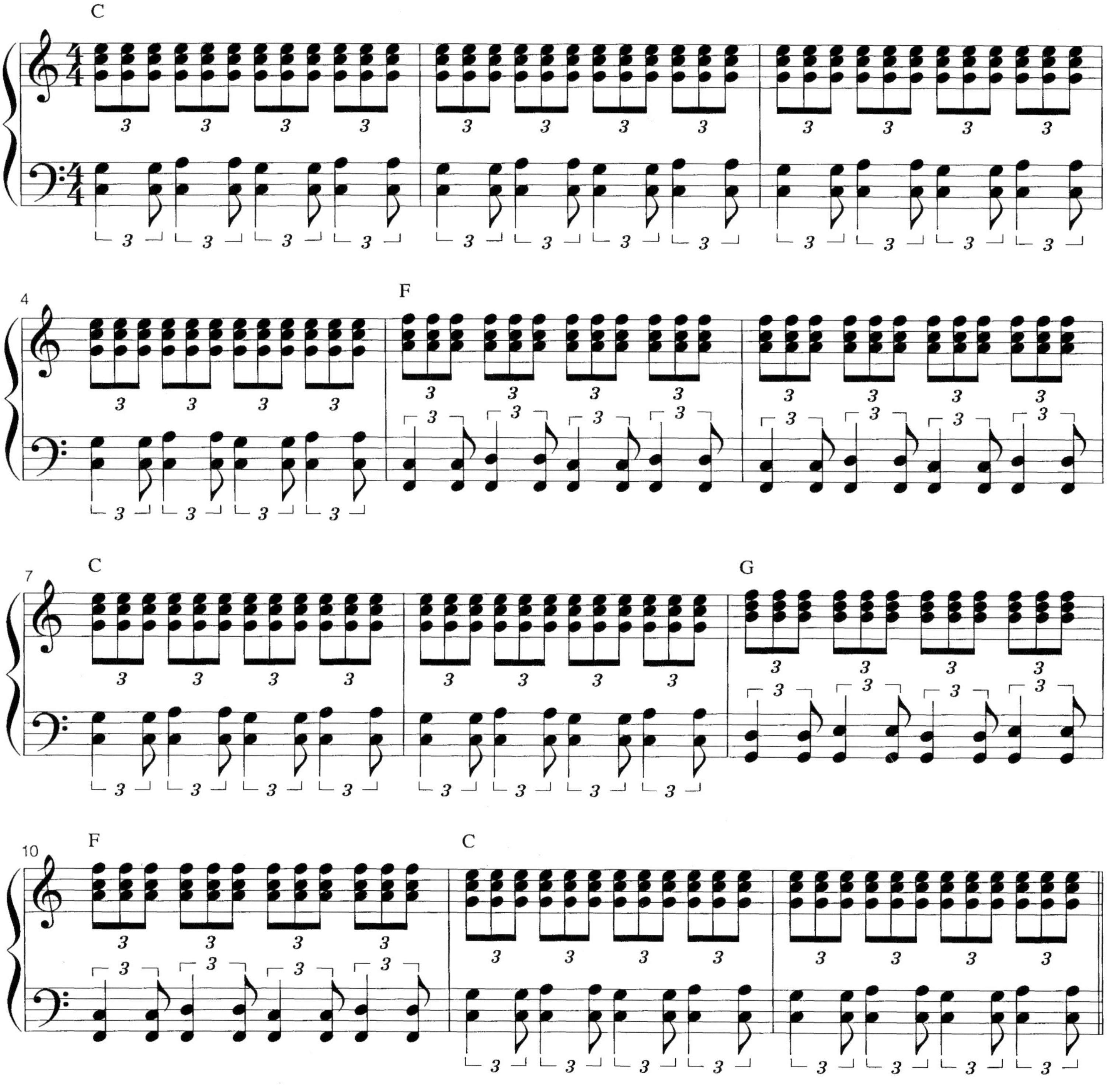

10 Turnaround

Insert at measure 12

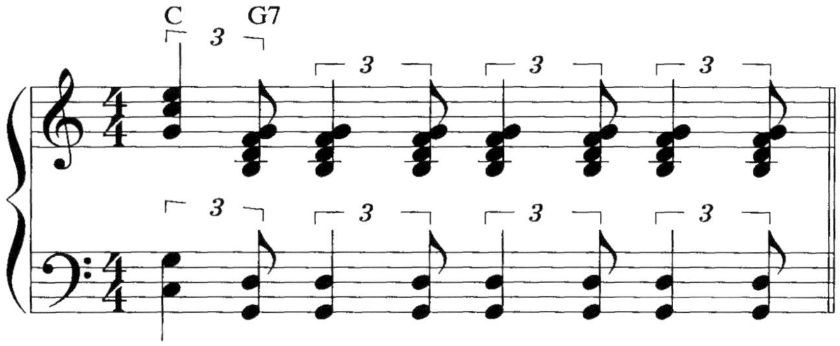

same as:

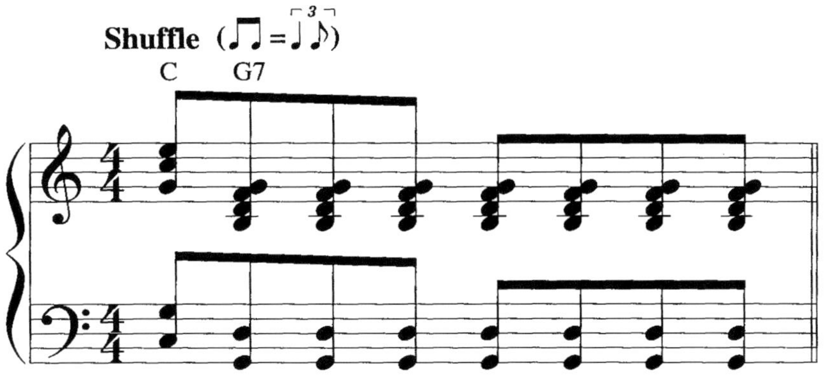

Shuffle Rhythm – Swing 8th's

12 Basic Shuffle Rhythm Pattern

13 Basic Shuffle Rhythm

Alternate Shuffle Rhythms

15 **1st Alternate**

16 **2nd Alternate**

17 **3rd Alternate**

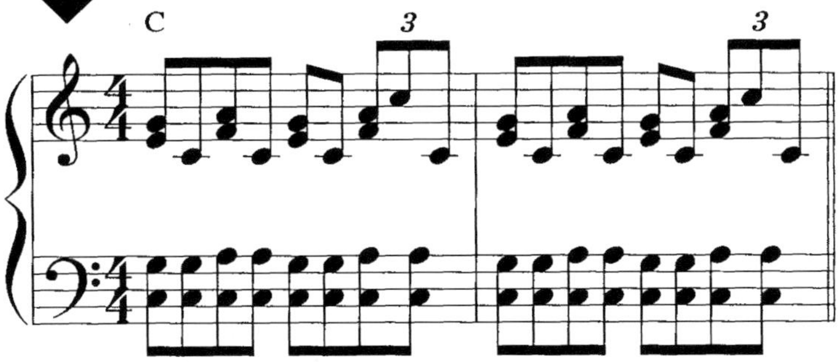

18 **4th Alternate**

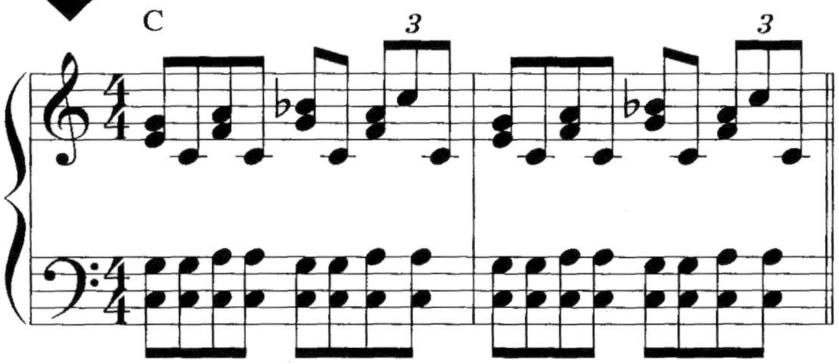

4th Alternate

4th Alternate

Syncopated Shuffle Rhythms

19 **1st Alternate**

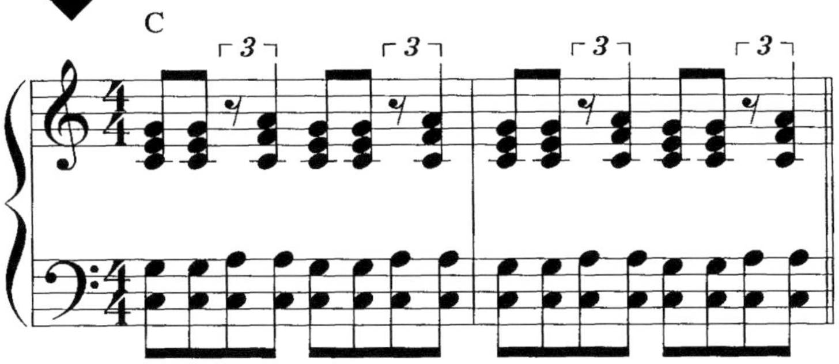

20 **2nd Alternate**

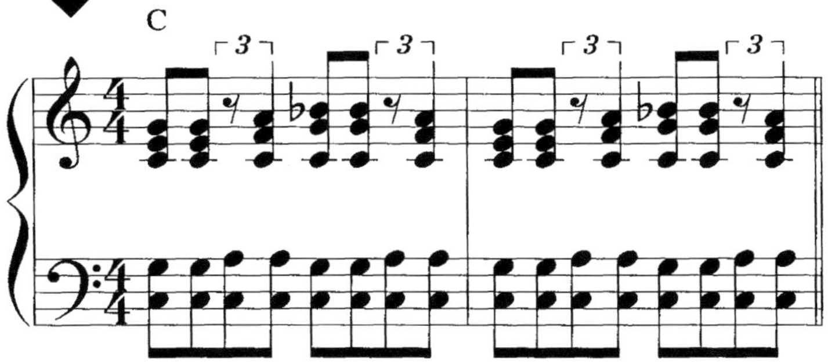

2nd Alternate (with Harmonic Variation)

21 3rd Alternate (The Quintuplet)

22 4th Alternate (Quintuplet & Triplet)

23 Modular 12 Bar Blues

(2 Verses)

[A] **Shuffle**

C
G
F
C
G7
End Rhythm Figure 1
B
Left Hand: with Rhythm Figure 1
C
F
C
G
F
C
G7

24 Solo Number 1

Shuffle (♫ = ♩♪ triplet)

Left Hand: with Rhythm Figure 1, 1st 10 measures

25 Variations

Example 1 – Trill

Insert at measures 2 and 4

Example 1 – Trill

Insert at measure 8

26 Example 3 – Ending

Insert at measure 12

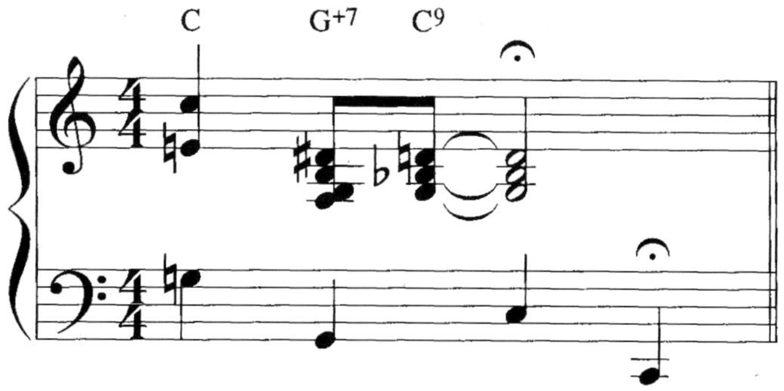

Solo Number 2

28 Diminished Chord Rhythms

Example 1

Example 2 with Trill

29 Solo Number 2

Shuffle

Left Hand: with Rhythm Figure 1

30 9th Chord Rhythm Solo

Variation

Insert at measure 12

32 Blues Scales

C Blues Scale / F Blues Scale

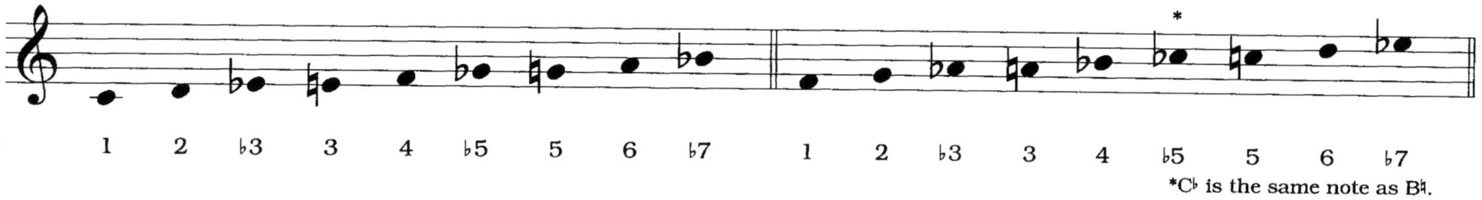

G Blues Scale / 33 C Minor Blues Scale

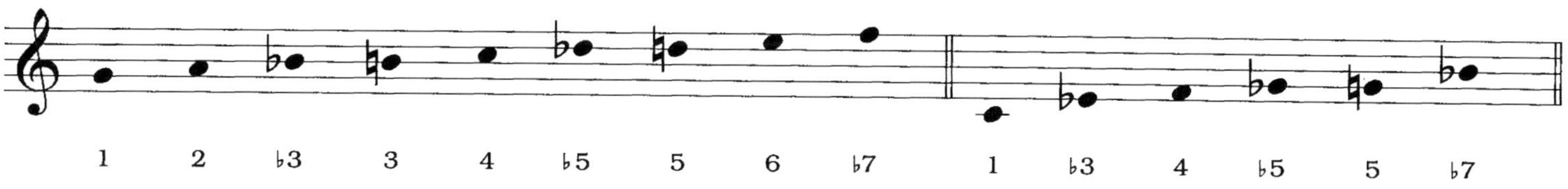

12 Bar C Minor Blues

Shuffle (♫ = ♩♪ triplet)

Left Hand: with Rhythm Figure 1

34 C Minor Blues Scale Solo

36 Solo Number 3

Shuffle (♫ = ♩♪ triplet)

Left Hand: with Rhythm Figure 1, 1st 11 measures

Slow Blues

38 Left Hand Patterns

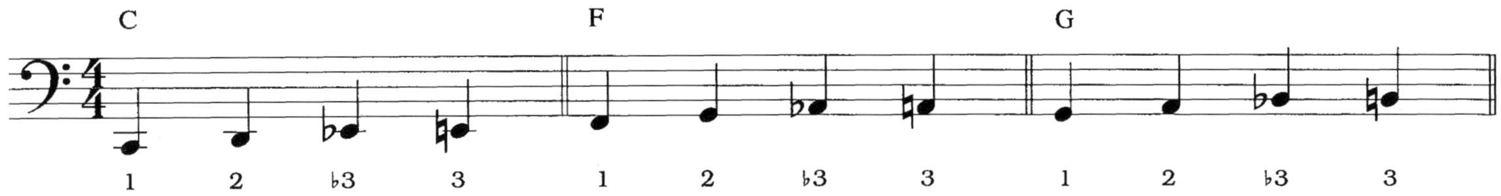

39 Slow Blues Verse

44 Slow Blues Chord Variations

Example 1 – 7th Chords
Insert for measures 1 through 3

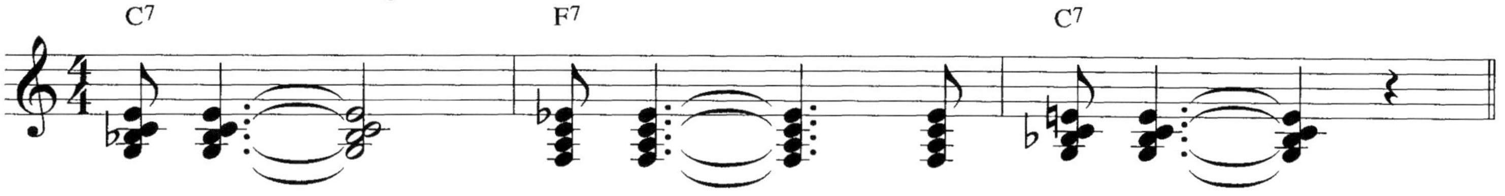

Example 2 – Triplets
Insert for measures 1 through 10

46 Using the Full Blues Scale

C Blues Scale

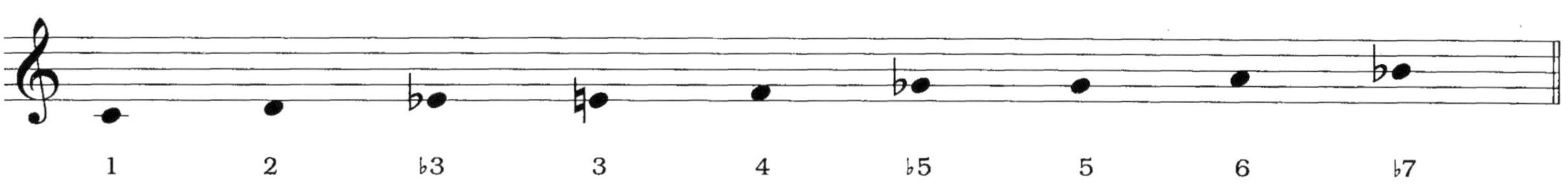

47 Common Blues Riff

Example 3

Insert for measures 1 through 5

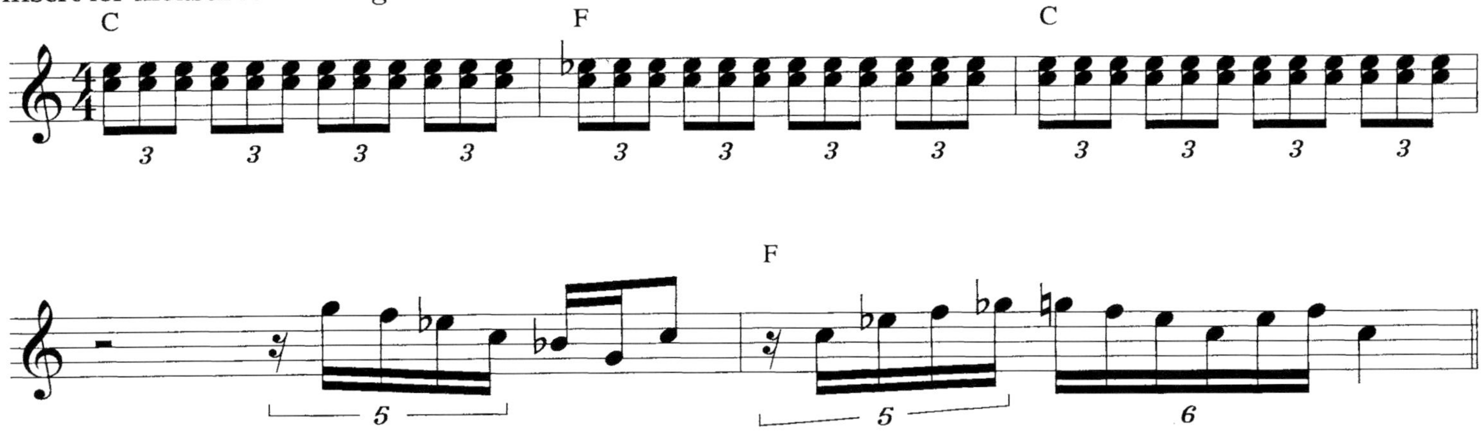

48 Improvisation Ideas

Example 1

Insert for measure 2

Example 2

Insert for measures 5 & 6

Example 3

Insert for measures 5 & 6

Example 4
Insert for measures 6, 7 & 8

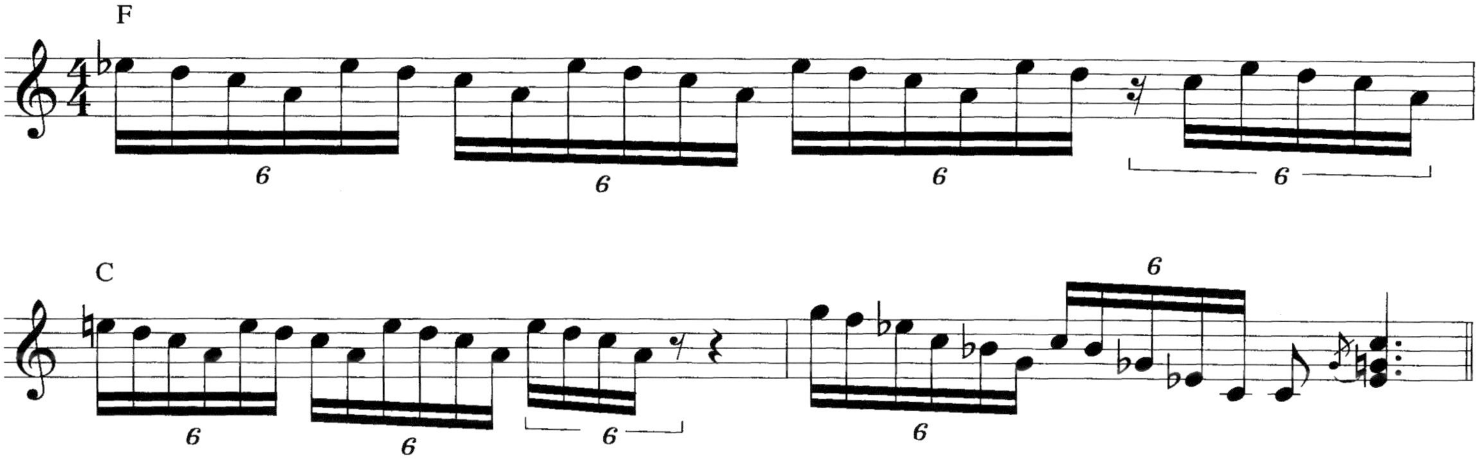

Example 5
Insert for measures 9 & 10

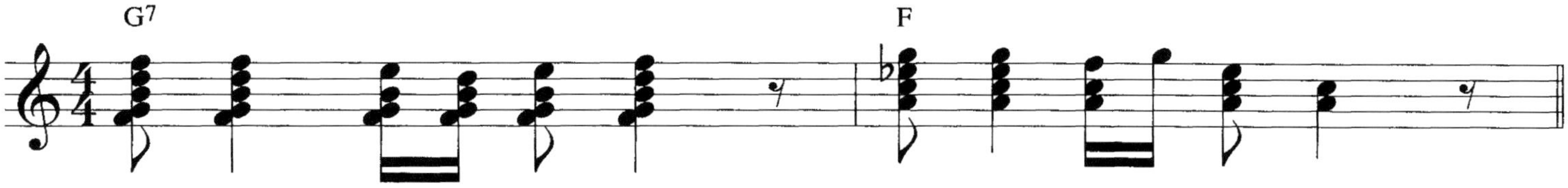

50 Slow Blues – Combining the Elements

A **Shuffle** (♫ = ♩♪ triplet)

Left Hand: with Rhythm Figure 2, 2 times

52 Tagging the Ending

Biography

"Mr. Cohen isn't the average hippie gone Wall Street. He's also a certifiably smokin' barrel-house rhumba boogie-woogie piano player in the James Booker/Professor Longhair/Dr. John vein."

David Bennet Cohen has been a professional musician for more than 50 years. Best known for his innovative keyboard playing as an original member of the '60s rock band, Country Joe and the Fish, he is an equally accomplished guitar player who has been involved in numerous music scenes throughout his varied career.

David began his musical education at the age of seven, studying classical piano for seven years. While studying the piano, he began to teach himself the guitar, beginning at the age of nine. When he was 14, he heard boogie-woogie piano for the first time and was hooked. Since then he has explored many different styles of blues and popular music. He was fortunate enough to have heard Otis Spann, Professor Longhair, Meade Lux Lewis and other masters of the genre perform live.

"What separates Cohen from a lot of other players is his unassuming ease behind the keys, and the ability to take that admiration past rote emulation, invoking the spirits of boogie-woogie, stride and blues piano greats without ever forcing things or just replicating other folks' licks."

Over the years, he has played and/or recorded with The Blues Project, Mick Taylor, The Luther Tucker Blues Band, Elvin Bishop, Melvin Van Peebles, Happy and Artie Traum, Arlen Roth, Eric Andersen, David Blue, Tim Hardin, Norton Buffalo, Jerry Miller (of Moby Grape), Steve Miller, Jimi Hendrix, Johnnie Winter, John Cippolina, Huey Lewis, Michael Bloomfield, Bob Weir, John Kahn and others.

As a solo performer, he has shared the bill with Country Joe McDonald, Kenny Rankin, Bonnie Raitt, Richard Thompson, Jerry Garcia, Leo Kottke, Rufus Thomas, Meat Loaf, Booker T., The Roaches, Kingfish and many others.

David has recorded several tutorial DVDs and downloads for Homespun Music Instruction, including "Blues and Rock Techniques for Hammond Organ" and a three-DVD set, "Learn to Play Blues Piano." He continues to perform in the New York City area, both solo and with the Former Members, a band whose members include Bruce Barthol (also formerly of Country Joe and the Fish), Roy Blumenfeld (of the Blues Project) and Greg Douglass (of the Steve Miller Band). He continues to teach, conduct workshops and play on recording sessions in the New York area and elsewhere.

"Cohen radiates the 88's impeccably."

All quotes from *CMJ New Music Report*

MORE GREAT *Blues Titles* FROM HOMESPUN®

RORY BLOCK TEACHES CLASSICS OF COUNTRY BLUES GUITAR

Here are some of the greatest country blues solos of all time, taught in phrase-by-phrase detail. Rory Block performs and breaks down these fingerstyle pieces by Willie Moore, Blind Willie McTell, Tommy Johnson, Mississippi John Hurt, Skip James and others.

00699065 Book/CD Pack..............................$19.95

HAPPY TRAUM TEACHES BLUES GUITAR

Beginning with the most basic strumming of a 12-bar blues pattern. Happy gradually starts adding fills, runs, turnarounds, bass rhythms and 'boogie woogie' walking bass patterns that make the basic blues progression come alive. All of these elements are notated in both notes and tab.

00841082 Book/CD Pack..............................$19.95

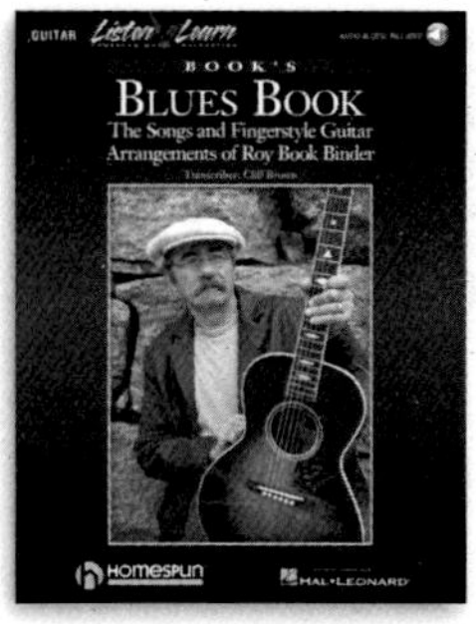

BOOK'S BLUES BOOK

A seasoned vet with a unique sound, Roy Book Binder has been singing, playing guitar, and writing songs since the '60s. This book/audio pack presents traditional and original blues tunes that have delighted his audiences for years.

00695808 Book/ Online Audio..........$19.99

ARTIE TRAUM TEACHES ESSENTIAL BLUES FOR ACOUSTIC GUITAR

Award-winning guitarist, songwriter, author and Taylor Guitars clinician Artie Traum explores essential blues techniques in fret-by-fret detail for both finger and flatpick styles.

00695805 Book/CD Pack.......$19.95

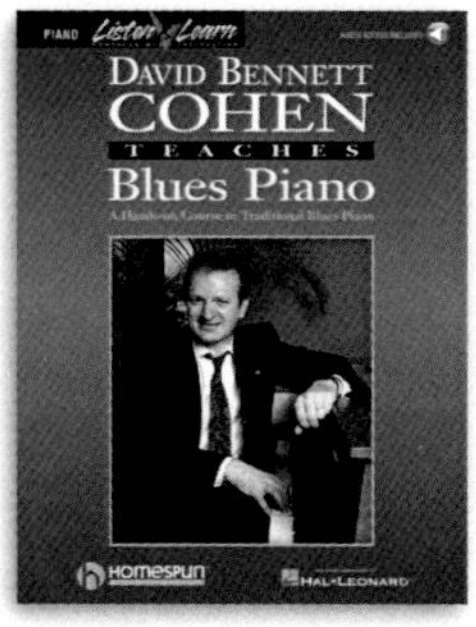

DAVID BENNETT COHEN TEACHES BLUES PIANO

David Cohen helps develop the powerful grooves beloved by blues and rock n' roll players alike. His unique step-by-step teaching method is modular, building logically on each preceding section.

00841084 Book/ Online Audio..........$19.95

RORY BLOCK TEACHES THE GUITAR OF ROBERT JOHNSON

DVD ONE

Award-winning contemporary blues singer and guitarist Rory Block completely demystifies the licks, runs, strums, bass lines, turnarounds and other important guitar elements that combine to make up the unique Robert Johnson sound. 113 minutes.

00641810 DVD..$29.95

EXPLORING THE GUITAR WITH KEB' MO'

Grammy-winner Keb' Mo' accompanies his songs with folk/blues fingerpicking, swampy slide licks, contemporary pop chords, and a touch of jazz. 110 minutes.

00642030 DVD............$29.95

SLIDE GUITAR FOR BLUES: LAP STYLE

taught by Bob Brozman

Bob Brozman teaches the funky blues tunes, cool riffs and adventurous improvisations that he pulls from his seemingly bottomless bag of tricks. 105 minutes.

00642023 DVD One.....$29.95

BLUES GUITAR ARRANGEMENTS IN DADGAD TUNING

taught by Al Petteway

One of our most musically inventive guitarists has devised a compelling and powerful way to use DADGAD tuning for playing a variety of fingerstyle blues instrumentals, from swampy Delta to the Piedmont, Big Bill to Doc Watson. 90 minutes.

00116374 DVD..$29.95

PUTTING THE "BLUES" INTO BLUEGRASS

taught by Steve Kaufman

Steve Kaufman brings his masterful skills to an engaging and user-friendly collection of twelve "bluesy" bluegrass standards that will serve any intermediate-level picker well in a jam, practice session or performance. Includes music and tab booklet. Early intermediate level.

00269444 DVD..$29.95

LEARN TO PLAY BLUES PIANO

taught by David Bennett Cohen

David Cohen systematically leads novice players through all the steps needed to play solid blues piano, showing the scales, chord theory, turnarounds, endings and licks that will quickly make anyone into a formidable player. 90 minutes.

00641760 DVD..$29.95

GREAT PIANO LESSONS: BLUES, GOSPEL AND COUNTRY STYLES

taught by David Bennett Cohen, Johnnie Johnson, Ethel Caffie-Austin, Dr. John & more

The powerful lessons on this DVD represent piano instruction at its very best. Each segment is taught by a legendary master of the keys and was chosen to provide a variety of traditional keyboard techniques. 1 hour, 20 minutes.

00157863 DVD..$19.95

ALSO AVAILABLE: OUTSTANDING BUNDLE PACKS!

HAPPY TRAUM – BLUES GUITAR

Includes the book/CD pack *Happy Traum Teaches Blues Guitar* and the DVD *Happy and Artie Traum's Easy Steps to Blues Guitar Jamming*, in one money-saving pack.

00642057 Book/CD/DVD Pack......................$44.95

ROBERT JOHNSON

This budget-saving bundle pack includes the book/CD pack *Robert Johnson – Signature Licks* snd the DVD *The Guitar Styles of Robert Johnson.*

00123285 Book/CD/DVD Pack......................$47.90

BOTTLENECK GUITAR

Includes the book *Bottleneck Blues Guitar* and the DVD *Great Bottleneck Blues Lessons* in one money-saving pack!

00139520 Book/DVD Pack............................$39.95

HAL•LEONARD®

www.halleonard.com

Prices, contents, and availability subject to change without notice.